BASEBALL LEGENDS

Hank Aaron
Grover Cleveland Alexander
Ernie Banks
Albert Belle
Johnny Bench
Yogi Berra
Barry Bonds
Roy Campanella
Roberto Clemente
Ty Cobb
Dizzy Dean
Joe DiMaggio
Bob Feller
Jimmie Foxx
Lou Gehrig
Bob Gibson
Ken Griffey, Jr.
Rogers Hornsby
Walter Johnson
Sandy Koufax
Greg Maddux
Mickey Mantle
Christy Mathewson
Willie Mays
Stan Musial
Satchel Paige
Mike Piazza
Cal Ripken, Jr.
Brooks Robinson
Frank Robinson
Jackie Robinson
Babe Ruth
Tom Seaver
Duke Snider
Warren Spahn
Willie Stargell
Frank Thomas
Honus Wagner
Ted Williams
Carl Yastrzemski
Cy Young

CHELSEA HOUSE PUBLISHERS

Baseball Legends

GREG MADDUX

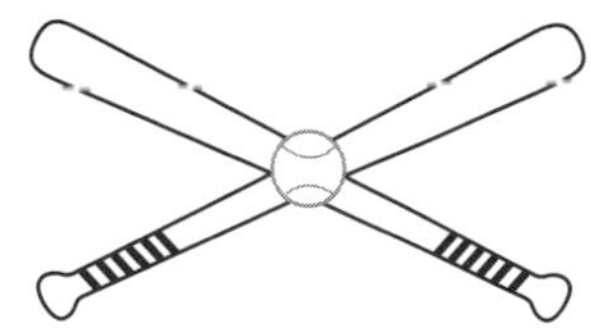

Norman L. Macht

Introduction by
Jim Murray

Senior Consultant
Earl Weaver

CHELSEA HOUSE PUBLISHERS
Philadelphia

The author is grateful to John Coleman, Dr. David K. Mulliken and Terry Mulliken of Pikeville, Kentucky; Pete Vonachen of the Peoria Chiefs; Mike Maddux; and all the players and coaches who helped me get this story right.

Cover photo credit: AP/Wide World Photo

Produced by Choptank Syndicate, Inc.

Editor and Picture Researcher: Norman L. Macht
Production Coordinator and Editorial Assistant: Mary E. Hull
Designer: Lisa Hochstein
Cover Designer: Alison Burnside

3 5 7 9 8 6 4 2

Library of Congress Cataloging-in-Publication Data

Macht, Norman L. (Norman Lee), 1929-
Greg Maddux / Norman L. Macht; introduction by Jim Murray; senior consultant, Earl Weaver.
p. cm. — (Baseball legends)
Includes bibliographical references (p.) and index.
ISBN 0-7910-4378-9 (hc)
1. Maddux, Greg, 1966- —Juvenile literature. 2. Baseball players—United States—Biography—Juvenile literature. 3. Atlanta Braves (Baseball team)—Juvenile literature. I. Title. II. Series.
GV865.M233M33 1997
796.357'092—dc21
[B] 97-5109
CIP
AC

CONTENTS

WHAT MAKES A STAR

Jim Murray

No one has ever been able to explain to me the mysterious alchemy that makes one man a .350 hitter and another player, more or less identical in physical makeup, hard put to hit .200. You look at an Al Kaline, who played with the Detroit Tigers from 1953 to 1974. He was pale, stringy, almost poetic-looking. He always seemed to be struggling against a bad case of mononucleosis. But with a bat in his hands, he was King Kong. During his career, he hit 399 home runs, rapped out 3,007 hits, and compiled a .297 batting average.

Form isn't the reason. The first time anybody saw Roberto Clemente step into the batter's box for the Pittsburgh Pirates, the best guess was that Clemente would be back in Double A ball in a week. He had one foot in the bucket and held his bat at an awkward angle—he looked as though he couldn't hit an outside pitch. A lot of other ballplayers may have had a better-looking stance. Yet they never led the National League in hitting in four different years, the way Clemente did.

Not every ballplayer is born with the ability to hit a curveball. Nor is exceptional hand-eye coordination the key to heavy hitting. Big league locker rooms are filled with players who have all the attributes, save one: discipline. Every baseball man can tell you a story about a pitcher who throws a ball faster than anyone has ever seen but who has no control on or *off* the field.

The Hall of Fame is full of people who transformed themselves into great ballplayers by working at the sport, by studying the game, and making sacrifices. They're overachievers—and winners. If you want to find them, just watch the World Series. Or simply read about New York Yankee great Lou Gehrig; Ted Williams, "the Splendid Splinter" of the Boston Red Sox; or the Dodgers' strikeout king Sandy Koufax.

A pitcher *should* be able to win a lot of ballgames with a 98-miles-per-hour fastball. But what about the pitcher who wins 20 games a year with a fastball so slow that you can catch it with your teeth? Bob Feller of the Cleveland Indians got into the Hall of Fame with a blazing fastball that glowed in the dark. National League star Grover Cleveland Alexander got there with a pitch that took considerably longer to reach the plate; but when it did arrive, the pitch was exactly where Alexander wanted it to be—and the last place the batter expected it to be.

There are probably more players with exceptional ability who didn't make it to the major leagues than there are who did. A number of great hitters, bored with fielding practice, had to be dropped from their team because their home-run production didn't make up for their lapses in the field. And then there are players like Brooks Robinson of the Baltimore Orioles, who made himself into a human vacuum cleaner at third base because he knew that working hard to become an expert fielder would win him a job in the big leagues.

A star is not something that flashes through the sky. That's a comet. Or a meteor. A star is something you can steer ships by. It stays in place and gives off a steady glow; it is fixed, permanent. A star works at being a star.

And that's how you tell a star in baseball. He shows up night after night and takes pride in how brightly he shines. He's Willie Mays running so hard his hat keeps falling off; Ty Cobb sliding to stretch a single into a double; Lou Gehrig, after being fooled in his first two at-bats, belting the next pitch off the light tower because he's taken the time to study the pitcher. Stars never take themselves for granted. That's why they're stars.

Braves
27
Braves
7

"BULL DOG" AND "MAD DOG"

"Did you try to hit him on purpose?"
— Cleveland pitcher Orel Hershiser

Orel "Bulldog" Hershiser took the mound for the Cleveland Indians in Game 5 of the 1995 World Series against Greg "Mad Dog" Maddux of the Atlanta Braves on October 26 in Cleveland. It was a cool, cloudy night, the temperature in the low 50s, the Cleveland crowd subdued but hopeful as their team faced a 3–1 deficit in the Series.

In the very first inning the two hardnosed hurlers came face to face on the mound. With two out and a man on second, Cleveland slugger Albert Belle walloped a long home run into the right field bleachers. It was the first first-inning home run Maddux had given up in five years.

As the cheering crowd of 43,595 settled down, veteran switch-hitter Eddie Murray stepped into the batter's box. Maddux zipped a fastball under his chin. Murray spun out of the way, then took a step toward Maddux and hollered a few words. At that, both teams swarmed out of the dugouts and pitchers poured from the bullpens. The umpires quickly stepped in and maintained order. No punches were thrown, just a rosin bag that hit Atlanta outfielder Luis Polonia in the back.

The Atlanta Braves celebrate their 1995 World Series victory at Fulton County Stadium after having come close to winning it three years in a row.

In the midst of the milling around, Bulldog and Mad Dog met on the mound.

"Did you try to hit him on purpose?" Hershiser asked.

"No," Maddux said. "I was trying to jam him."

Knowing that Maddux had near-perfect control, Hershiser said, "You can do better than that. Remember, I'm going to have the ball, too."

The two aces glared at each other with mutual respect. Each got the other's message.

Hershiser, who had never lost in seven post-season decisions with the Los Angeles Dodgers,

Sitting on the bench wearing glasses, Maddux may look more like a librarian than an athlete, but when he puts in his contact lenses and takes the mound, he is a fierce competitor.

had been dubbed Bulldog by Dodgers manager Tommy Lasorda. He was a tenacious, intelligent pitcher who earned his nickname by battling every hitter with every pitch.

Maddux, a little guy with glasses who looked more like a choirboy, had been called Mad Dog for as long as he could remember. Through Little League, high school, the minor leagues and the big leagues, he rarely missed a start, loved the challenge of competition and hated to lose. Like Hershiser, he pitched as much with his brain as his arm.

Neither right-hander hesitated to throw inside, brush back a hitter, and take command of the plate.

The two teams brought different histories into this confrontation. The Indians had not been to a World Series in 41 years. Winners of 100 games in the curtailed 144-game schedule, they had built a powerhouse, hitting 207 home runs. Led by Albert Belle, the first player ever to blast 50 home runs and 50 doubles in a season, they had run away from the American League Central Division, finishing 31 games ahead of the pack. They had swept the Red Sox, then defeated a tough Seattle team in the playoffs. Hershiser had beaten the Mariners twice to win the ALCS MVP Award.

The Atlanta Braves had won more games in the 1990s than any other team. But they still felt like losers, because they had failed to win the big one each year. The sports world kept reminding them of it, comparing them to the Buffalo Bills of the NFL, who went to four Super Bowls in a row without a victory.

In 1991 the Braves had lost Games 6 and 7 in extra innings to the Minnesota Twins. In 1992 an 11th-inning loss in Game 6 sent them home from Toronto. Each of their last seven World Series losses had been by one run. Their critics called them chokers.

That winter they had signed the best pitcher in baseball, Greg Maddux, a free agent who had won the Cy Young Award in 1992 with the Chicago Cubs. The Braves already had the best pitching staff in the National League, headed by Tommy Glavine, John Smoltz and Steve Avery. They figured that Maddux would put them over the top.

Maddux won 20 games for them in 1993 and another Cy Young Award for himself. But he lost the deciding game of the playoffs to the Phillies, and the Braves watched the World Series on TV. The players' strike canceled the 1994 World Series; they had to wait another year for a chance to vindicate themselves and shake the losers' label.

From the start of the strike-delayed 1995 season, the Braves' only goal was to win the World Series. Nothing short of that, no individual awards, no record-setting performances, would satisfy them or their critics and fans. They breezed through the NL East, winning by 21 games. Maddux won 19 and lost only 2. Then they polished off the Colorado Rockies and Cincinnati Reds in the expanded playoffs, and here they were again, carrying the losers' monkey on their backs into another World Series.

'Individually, I've accomplished more than I ever thought possible," Maddux said. "That doesn't matter to me anymore. The thing that's important to me is . . . to get a World Series ring and just stick it on a wall somewhere. And then, whoever comes over to the house can look at it. I would like that."

The benches clear after a high inside pitch from Greg Maddux sent Cleveland's Eddie Murray spinning out of the way in the first inning of Game 5 of the 1995 World Series in Cleveland. Rival pitchers Maddux and Orel Hershiser exchange words near the mound.

Both Hershiser and Maddux were rested and well-prepared for Game 1 in Atlanta under clear skies and 61-degree weather on October 21. Cleveland scored a run in the first without a hit. Speedy leadoff batter Kenny Lofton was safe on an infield error, stole second and third, and scored on a groundout.

Atlanta's Fred McGriff led off the second with a home run to tie the score. From then until the seventh both pitchers mowed down the opposition like a reaper cutting hay. Maddux gave up a single in the fifth and never walked a batter. The first to blink was Hershiser, who walked the first two batters in the seventh and left the game. The Braves scored two runs without a ball being hit out of the infield.

Maddux gave up his second hit in the ninth; another error led to the Indians' second run, but Maddux finished the game a 3-2 winner. Seldom had a pitcher so dominated such a power-packed lineup in a World Series. His first pitch had been a strike to 22 of the 30 batters he faced. Only four fly balls had been hit by Cleveland's sluggers.

The Braves won three of the first four games before Maddux and Hershiser squared off again in Cleveland. This time the Tribe was ready for Maddux; they had studied videos of Game 1 intensely and made adjustments in their stances and strategies at the plate.

After Belle's first-inning home run and the duster to Murray, the Indians were fired up, determined to "get a piece" of Maddux. In the chilly wind, Maddux was not as sharp as usual—he actually walked THREE batters—but he fought them off until the sixth while Atlanta tied the score. Then the Indians got to him for a walk and three hits to take a 4–2 lead. They added another in the eighth off a relief pitcher. Atlanta came back with two in the ninth, but they fell short, 5–4. Their victory celebration would have to wait.

Back in Atlanta two nights later, Tommy Glavine chased the monkey off their backs for good by pitching a masterful one-hit shutout. David Justice's home run was the only score in the game.

Players who have been there agree that "nothing beats that high you get at the moment of clinching that championship. When you see guys piling up out on the field and swarming all over each other, that's the utmost you can feel in sports. It doesn't have to sink in later. That's it. That's the top, right then and there."

Glavine, whose two wins in the Series made him the MVP, said later, "We've accomplished a lot since 1991, but we didn't win a championship. None of us wanted . . . to go through the winter with another close defeat hanging over our heads."

A few weeks later Greg Maddux won an unprecedented fourth consecutive Cy Young trophy, and people began to recognize the guy in the glasses who looked like a librarian and couldn't throw enough heat to impress a radar gun as one of the best pitchers in history.

MGM

2

THE KID BROTHER

"If I can't win, I don't want to play."
— Greg Maddux

Gregory Alan Maddux was born on April 14, 1966 in San Angelo, Texas, where his father was an Air Force finance and accounting officer. Like most military families, the Madduxes led a nomadic life. Greg's brother, Mike, had been born almost five years earlier in Dayton, Ohio. Their sister, Terri, 7, was born in Anchorage, Alaska.

Soon after Greg was born, his father, Dave Maddux, was transferred to Thailand during the Vietnam War. The children and their mother, Linda, went to stay with Greg's grandparents in Westport, Indiana, a small town midway between Indianapolis and Cincinnati. This was Reds territory, and Greg was indoctrinated into the gospel of the Big Red Machine. The Reds' Pete Rose became his hero.

Maddux's home town, Las Vegas, Nevada, is known for its glamorous hotels, entertainment and casinos. The MGM Grand is the world's largest, with more than 5,000 rooms. But Las Vegas also has homes, schools, libraries, churches and parks like any other town.

By the time Greg was 7, they had lived in Minot, North Dakota; Riverside, California; and Madrid, Spain. During their three years in Spain, they lived, worked, played and went to school on the Air Force base with other Americans. They had their own gym and baseball field on the base.

When brothers are 13 and 8, that age difference often causes a big gap between them. A little brother four or five years younger may be considered a nuisance by the older boy. That was not the case with Mike and Greg. They were pals. Their parents could be certain of two things: wherever Mike was, Greg was with him. And whatever ball was in season—baseball, basketball, football—they had it in their hands.

The brothers even teamed up in teasing their sister, coming up with the nastiest things they could say and do to disgust her, then collapsing in laughter.

Whenever they went looking for a pick-up game, Mike always chose Greg first to be on his team. It was not just because Greg was his brother; he was a good athlete. Greg was also a fierce competitor who hated to lose. When they were alone, they made up their own games.

"He and I played Whiffle ball together," Mike said. "You got one pitch. If it was a ball, you walked. If it was a strike, you were out. You got one out per inning, and three innings was a game. Whoever won four games first won the series, like the World Series. A series took about 20 minutes.

"Well, we'd start out with whoever won two out of three series was the winner for the day. But if I won, then Greg would say, 'Make it three out of five.' If I won three, then he'd want it to be four out of seven, then five out of nine, then the best out of 11, then 13, then 15—anything to keep him from losing. We'd probably still be playing today if he didn't win, so eventually I would fold so the game would be over and he could go home and say he won."

When their father got off work, he would play catch, hit grounders, and pitch batting practice for them. A fast-pitch softball pitcher, he had idolized Mickey Mantle as a teenager. Aware of how Mantle's father had trained his son to be a ballplayer, Dave Maddux vowed to do the same with his boys. He encouraged them to pitch to a location, rather than just rearing back and throwing as hard as they could. Wherever his father held the mitt, Greg became adept at hitting the target.

Maddux also honed the boys' mental skills, calling out game situations they had to respond to. As a result, when they were ready for Little League, they were far ahead of the other kids in the fundamentals and understanding of the game.

Greg developed a phenomenal memory. In the card game Concentration, he knew after one glance where every card was. That mental flypaper would later be used to trap big league hitters.

Greg picked up his first nickname in the third grade. "One day the teacher gave out a sample paper of how to do homework," Dave Maddux recalled. "At the top of the paper it said, 'My name is . . . ' and it had the name Nat Yates on it. Well, after that Greg put 'Nat Yates' on all his papers. Ever since then we've called him Nate."

There were enough boys on the base to form a Little League. Greg was the best athlete, so he pitched. But he really enjoyed hitting more. He had remained a Reds fan; when he batted, he imitated the stances and swings of Pete Rose and Joe Morgan and the other stars of the Cincinnati world champions of 1975 and 1976.

There were fewer boys of Mike's age on the base, so he had to go across the city to play in an older league. But they had very little contact with the Spanish people, and the only thing they learned to say in Spanish was to ask for "pipas" when they went to buy sunflower seeds.

Greg was 10 when the family moved from Spain to Las Vegas, Nevada. For the first time they were living in a city, not on a military base. They went to public schools for the first time and were exposed to the "real" world—Las Vegas version.

Created as a resort in the middle of the desert, Las Vegas is known for its glamorous big hotels, entertainment stars and gambling casinos. But behind all the glitter and excitement of downtown, thousands of families lived in neighborhoods with schools, libraries, churches, supermarkets and baseball fields like any other town.

Greg Maddux idolized his big brother, Mike, shown here with his first major league team, the Phillies. On September 26, 1986, the two brothers started against each other for the first time in the big leagues. Greg won that encounter, 8–3.

Their arrival in 1976 coincided with the glory years of the University of Nevada–Las Vegas basketball team. The Running Rebels of UNLV were routinely running up 100 points a game. They went to the 1977 NCAA Final Four but lost in the semi-finals.

Mike and Greg set up a full court—about 15 feet long—in their garage and imitated the Running Rebels playing Nerf ball. "We'd set the timer for a five-minute game," Mike said, "with an implied shot clock of about three seconds. Take a couple steps, pull up, shoot, run the other way, pull up, shoot, turn and burn and have a real sweat going."

Mike pitched for Rancho High School. When he graduated in 1979, the Reds drafted him, but he decided he was not ready for pro ball. He wanted to learn what it was like to be away from home, and went to the University of Texas – El Paso, where he pitched for three years. In June 1982 the Phillies drafted him.

Greg was then 16, going to Valley High School and working at Wendy's when he was not playing ball. He was unflappable even then. "It's not hard work," he said. "People act like it is. A lot of people hated working there. You've got to go there saying you'll have a good time, and you will."

His father, now retired from the Air Force, was a poker dealer at one of the downtown hotels. His mother worked as a dispatcher for the Henderson County police department.

Pitching for Valley High, Greg made the All-State team as a junior and senior. But his easygoing, relaxed attitude before games confounded his coach, who took it as a lack of seriousness. "Before big games I'd be as tight as could be," coach Rodger Fairless said, "and he'd be so loose he'd be horsing around."

The T-shirt Greg wore under his uniform was more revealing of the real Greg. It read, "If I can't win, I don't want to play."

Las Vegas had a team in the AAA Pacific Coast League. Greg and his buddies went to the Stars' games and had a good time razzing and hollering at the players on both the home and visiting teams.

Greg began to get publicity and attract big league scouts. When scouts look at pitchers, they look for good athletes, and Greg was clearly an all-around athlete. They noted his arm and smooth delivery and composure. But he was a skinny little guy, standing 5-foot-10 and weighing about 150. Most teams prefer strapping six-footers who weigh 200 and can throw 95 mph. They turned their attention to the bigger, more impressive-looking pitchers in the state tournament. Some questioned Greg's endurance and thought he would be better off going to college where he could grow and mature before trying pro ball.

But there was one scout who thought differently.

3

LIFE IN THE LOW MINORS

"Too small to play in the big leagues."
— Scouts' reports

Gene Handley was a 5-foot-10, 155-pound infielder who had "a cup of coffee" (a brief stay) in the big leagues 40 years earlier. Like Greg Maddux, Handley had an older brother who had set an example and lasted 10 years in the majors even though he was only 5-foot-7. Handley knew you didn't have to be big to be a big leaguer. In baseball, brains and heart could count for more than brawn. The size of the fight in the man was more important than the size of the man in the fight.

Handley, the veteran scouting supervisor for the Chicago Cubs, came to Las Vegas to look over another Valley High pitcher, Mike Greer, in the 1983 state championship tournament. Greer was okay, he thought, but when a little junior named Maddux relieved him in the fifth inning, Handley sat up and took notice. He saw a fine athlete with a good arm and a smooth, easy delivery.

Blessed with an arm that seemed built for pitching, Greg threw with a natural motion that made the ball dip and dart when it got to home plate—up, down, in, out—depending on how he gripped it. A below-average fastball that moves can be more baffling to a hitter than a 95-mph fastball that is straight as a rope. That movement,

Greg Maddux began his professional career in this ballpark in Pikeville, Kentucky, of the Appalachian Rookie League. The grandstand, which holds 250, was seldom filled.

and Greg's ability to throw each pitch just where he wanted it to go, impressed Handley.

The title game was played on the UNLV diamond. To the Valley High kids, that was the big time. Greg hit a grand slam and Valley High won. Handley told his area scout, Doug Mapson, to keep an eye on Maddux in his senior year.

Mapson showed up for Valley's opening game in the spring of 1984 only to see the leadoff batter bash Greg's second pitch for a home run. But Mapson looked beyond that and saw a youngster who could reach down for something extra and throw a heater when he needed it, who could run, throw, hit, and field his position. In short, Greg Maddux knew what he was doing and was in command on the mound.

Of course, other scouts saw the same things. But many questioned if Greg would ever grow enough to endure the long, hot major league seasons. A few recommended Greg to their teams, which put him low on their wish lists. Other scouts, who knew their bosses preferred 6-foot-5 power pitchers as raw material, did not want to risk looking foolish by recommending the 150-pounder, so they wrote "Too small to play in the big leagues" on their reports.

Mapson got acquainted with Greg and his family. He told them he would urge the Cubs to select him in the June draft, but not to expect to be a first-round choice. Greg thought he had a future in baseball—he had reluctantly given up working out with the huge UNLV basketball players who might deal him a crushing injury—but he did not sit by the telephone waiting for the call. He was in Hawaii on a senior class trip when the Cubs made their first pick a 6-foot-4, 220-pound college southpaw, Drew Hall. Then

Mapson held his breath, hoping no other team would pick Greg before the Cubs' second turn. Thirty other players were selected before the Cubs took Greg.

Greg signed for a bonus of $85,000, which he vowed not to touch until he made it to the big leagues. He reported to the Cubs' mini-camp along with the highly-touted Drew Hall (who would win only five games in the major leagues) and another college pitcher, Jamie Moyer, who would make it to the Cubs just ahead of Greg.

"Greg was young, energetic, and green," Moyer recalled. "But nothing really fazed him or amazed him. He seemed to be on an even keel from the start."

The most popular lady among gamblers in Las Vegas was Lady Luck, and Greg seemed blessed with good luck in everything he played, from cards to slot machines to golf. But when it came to baseball, he began his career with the attitude: "Dude, I'm a firm believer in making your own luck."

The Cubs assigned Greg to Pikeville, Kentucky in the Class A Appalachian Rookie League. He flew to the nearest airport at Lexington, 150 miles away, where Terry Mulliken, the son of the club president, met him. On the way to Pikeville, Greg confided that he would have gone to college if the Cubs had not come up with the right money. "He was very well-spoken," Terry recalled, "and knew what he wanted in life. It was as if he planned his life the way he planned for a game, and thought about how he was going to do it."

The transition from being a high school or college player to a professional requires a tremendous mental adjustment. Many young players cannot make it. They had been big heroes in their home towns; now suddenly they were surrounded by—and competing with—equally big stars. There were five all-state quarterbacks on the Pikeville Cubs that year.

"There is a big difference between playing for fun and playing professionally," Mike Maddux said. "Instead of one or two games a week, you're playing every day through a long schedule."

They rode buses for hours on week-long road trips that seemed to stretch for months, with nothing to do in the small towns during the day. Buses broke down in the middle of the night on winding mountain roads. Many players were away from home for the first time. Homesickness cut short many a promising career.

Players from varied backgrounds came together to form a team. Some arrived wearing designer boots and clothes and carrying fancy luggage. Others, like Greg, wore blue jeans. To college stars and boys from big cities, life in Pikeville took some adapting. A town of 4,700 in the eastern tip of Kentucky, Pikeville had no pool hall, no malls, one movie theater. The players lived in the dorms of a small local college. There was little to do during the day but watch soap operas on television or play cards until it was time to go to the ballpark. The change in life style was more difficult for the black rookies in small all-white towns like Pikeville.

Many rookies coming out of big cities and college baseball programs have a hard time adjusting to the spartan conditions in the lower minor leagues, like the Pikeville dugout. The adjacent high school locker room, which served as a clubhouse, was better than some other facilities in the league.

But the townspeople welcomed the players and tried to entertain them. On days off, Dr. David K. Mulliken, president of the Pikeville club, invited the team to his home for picnics. They swam in his pool and played touch football.

The team played on the high school field and dressed in the school locker room. The fans had raised the money to build a 250-seat grandstand behind home plate. It was seldom filled; the average attendance was about 150. Clubhouses were tiny, with two or three showerheads, undependable hot water, and skimpy towels. Some fields were well kept, some were not. Some had no grass in the infield. In one coal mining town, Paintsville, the setting sun in center field shone right in the hitters' eyes. They had to stop the game and hoist a huge net in center field to block the sun until it went down.

None of this bothered Greg Maddux. He missed his high school girlfriend, Kathy, but his nomadic life in a military family had accustomed him to moving around, fitting in, making new friends and losing them. Nor were small towns alien to him; he had visited his grandparents often in Westport, Indiana, a town half the size of Pikeville.

"Greg was a cool customer," Dr. Mulliken said, "friendly but not a party person. He enjoyed swimming in the pool and playing touch football, but he was there to play baseball and to learn. He took the game seriously, and was very professional, well beyond his years."

Greg won 6 and lost 2 in the short season. It earned him a promotion to Peoria, Illinois in the advanced A Midwest League in 1985. Greg was confident in his ability, but he knew he had to advance one step at a time.

Chiefs

Peoria Chiefs Alumni

4

PITCHING INSIDE

"That's the batboy."
— Cubs manager Gene Michael

In the lower minor leagues, most hard-throwing pitchers lack control. They walk a lot of batters. But they are also helped by inexperienced hitters who swing at bad pitches, or are overpowered by anybody throwing real gas. Greg was smaller than the rest of the pitchers, and he did not throw an eye-popping fastball. But he stood out because he had exceptional poise and a smooth delivery. He seemed to know what he was doing. And he threw strikes.

Peoria manager Pete Mackanin picked Greg to pitch the 1985 Midwest League opener. "Greg was cool with an inner confidence," he observed. "That demeanor is something you can't teach. Either a person has it or they don't. He had no pretense, no excess baggage, and was very mature for his age."

When Mackanin asked him if he had learned anything in his first year of pro ball, Greg said, "I thought there would be a lot of trick plays. We had more in high school."

Greg was also tough and aggressive on the field, sending hitters spinning in the dirt when it suited his purposes. One night he witnessed what that could lead to.

Few of the thousands of minor league players go on to have long careers in the big leagues. Three Peoria Chiefs who succeeded are, from left: Greg Maddux, Rafael Palmeiro, and Mark Grace.

Quad Cities was in town. Tim Rice, pitching for the Peoria Chiefs, threw too close to one batter and hit him. As the bruised batter jogged to first base, he yelled something at Rice. In the next half inning, a Chiefs batter was thrown out at first on a ground ball. As he passed in front of the visitors' dugout, he did some jawing. They answered back. Words flew, then the visitors stormed out of the dugout and the battle began. Soon there were three or four separate fights raging on the field.

Unlike most baseball fights—a little pushing and shoving and a lot of talking—this one was "real and it was ugly," according to Quad Cities outfielder Jeff Manto. "They were kicking with their spikes, and punches were thrown."

"They were using bats and kicking guys in the head," Quad Cities manager Bill Lachemann recalled.

It took more than 30 minutes to break it up. But it was not over. "One of our guys, Miguel Garcia, was thrown out of the game," Manto said. "He had to pass the Peoria bullpen down the left field line to get to the clubhouse. He said something to the guys in the bullpen and they jumped him and it started all over again in left field."

It took another half hour to restore order again.

The 150-pound Maddux stayed out of the donnybrook. It was the biggest baseball fight he ever saw, but it did not deter him. He started the next night and kept the brushback pitch in his game plan.

The owner of the Chiefs, Pete Vonachen, took an interest in his young players, who lived in furnished apartments, usually three to an apartment. After a game they would get a sandwich at Rocky's Hitching Post or Sully's restaurant. On the road they received $11.50 a day meal money. But they were visiting some cities where it cost more than that to eat. Unlike the major leagues, there were no spreads of food in the clubhouse after a game, and they were lucky to find a fast food place still open late at night. Some kids lived on peanut butter and jelly sandwiches.

Peoria players who agreed to make a personal appearance at a school or hospital or civic club were promised a good lunch by Vonachen. He never had any problem getting volunteers. On a stormy night, when it looked as if they might not play, the players prayed for a rainout. They knew that Vonachen would come into the clubhouse and take them all out for a spaghetti dinner.

The average salary was about $700 a month and the players were usually broke. When Kathy came to visit him, Greg bought an old car for about $150. But he had trouble getting it started whenever he wanted to use it. Told he needed a new battery, Greg said, "I don't have the money for a battery." So Vonachen bought him one.

For some college stars, the playing conditions were a big comedown. Six-footers bumped their heads on low dugout roofs. Clubhouses were little better than the Appalachian League

Just one year out of high school, Maddux pitched the opening game for the Peoria Chiefs in 1985. Peoria manager Pete Mackanin remembers him as "cool with an inner confidence . . . something you can't teach. Either a person has it or they don't."

facilities. The 12-hour bus rides were exhausting. Greg was used to the dry desert heat of Las Vegas, and the muggy humidity of the midwestern summer wore him down. He was 11–4 in mid-July, then wilted and won only 2 and lost 5 the rest of the way.

Greg got his first taste of being on a winning team that falls short of total victory; Peoria won the Southern Division by 9 games, but lost to Kenosha for the league championship, 3 games to 1. He was drilled for 5 runs in four innings in his only playoff start.

Greg began the 1986 season at Pittsfield, Massachusetts in the Class AA Eastern League and finished it in the major leagues with the Chicago Cubs. After completing and winning four of his eight starts at Pittsfield—two of them shutouts—he was promoted to the Iowa Cubs in the AAA American Association, where he won 10 and lost only 1.

His intensity on the mound and his obsession with perfection set Maddux at war with himself. When a pitch did not go exactly where he aimed it, even if it struck the batter out, he would turn toward the outfield, hold his glove in front of his face, and yell into it. His catcher at Iowa, Steve Roadcap, recalled, "He was very emotional on the field. But he never let it affect his pitching. He never blew up. He'd get so intense out there

Peoria Chiefs owner Pete Vonachen, for whom the Chiefs Stadium is named, took an active interest in his Cubs farmhands, taking them out to dinner when a game was rained out and sometimes lending them money in emergencies.

I would try to break the tension by going out to him and talking about something—anything else other than the game."

It was almost as if Maddux was two different people. He would clown around in the clubhouse, wear a Mickey Mouse cap and a Bugs Bunny T-shirt, looking and acting like a juvenile Clark Kent. But between the chalk lines he became Superman, a combative warrior bent on destroying every hitter's timing, dignity and batting average.

Maddux was still learning about pitching, but his ability to study hitters was so far ahead of the other pitchers, they listened like students whenever he talked pitching. And he could talk it by the hour.

The Cubs called him up to Chicago September 1. He was 20, had grown a little and added a few pounds, but still not enough to look like a big league pitcher. A coach took him for a clubhouse boy and almost asked him to fetch a pair of socks for him, before deciding to get them himself.

Greg got dressed and went into the Cubs' dugout. The manager, Gene Michael, was standing in front of the dugout with a coach, John Vukovich. Vukovich said to Michael, "Aren't you going to say hello to your new pitcher?"

"Where is he?"

Vukovich pointed into the dugout. "Right there."

Michael turned and looked. "I don't see anybody."

"He's right in front of you," Vukovich said.

"That's the batboy," Michael said.

"That's your new pitcher," Vukovich replied.

5

THE TURNING POINT

"If you get beat enough trying to do something, you eventually change."
— Greg Maddux

Most pitching staffs have a few veterans the younger hurlers look up to for advice and inspiration. In 1986 the Cubs had three: Rick Sutcliffe, Dennis Eckersley and Lee Smith. Smith, a 6-foot-5, dominating closer, called Maddux "Batboy" but soon gained a healthy respect for him.

"You never know when a young pitcher comes up how he'll turn out," he observed. "You can't look at any of them and say, 'This guy is going to be a Cy Young winner.' Some people said Maddux wouldn't last because he wasn't that big. But he had a lot of poise, and he just kept getting smarter and smarter. He had awesome work habits, always in the training room working on his legs.

"I never dreamed he would do all he did when I saw him that first year. But a lot of success is in the individual—how much he wants it."

Nobody awed or intimidated Maddux when he arrived on the scene looking like the batboy. Just two years out of high school, "he made his presence known," recalled Johnny Oates, then a Cubs coach. "He would tell it like it was from the first day, wouldn't take anything off anybody.

The first time Maddux appeared in a Cubs uniform, the manager, Gene Michael, thought he was the batboy. But Maddux quickly proved he belonged by pitching a complete game in his first start, an 11–3 win over the Cincinnati Reds.

Don Zimmer managed the Cubs from 1988 to 1991. Even after leaving the Cubs to coach for other teams, he still called Maddux the best pitcher in either league.

He'd get on himself more than on others. You'd think this little sawed-off guy was popping off, but he wasn't. It was like: 'do it right; put something into it.'"

The Cubs were in fifth place when Maddux joined them on September 1, 1986, so manager Gene Michael did not hesitate to use the rookie. Two days later, Michael sent Maddux in to start the 18th inning of a 6–6 game against Houston. With one out, Billy Hatcher hit a home run to give the Astros the lead, which they held. Maddux pitched one inning and had his first major league loss.

One day in Cincinnati, Maddux and Jamie Moyer, a pair of skinny rookies, were playing pepper behind the batting cage. Reds' manager Pete Rose walked by and looked at them and said, "Don't they feed you guys?"

Maddux showed him; he made his first start and pitched a complete game win over the Reds, 11–3. He also had two hits.

Maddux won one more game that year, and it was a memorable one. On September 29 he started against his brother, Mike, who was with the Phillies. Neither Maddux had a hit that day; Greg won the game, 8–3.

From the start, Maddux was determined to pitch inside and brush back hitters, and he let everybody know it. When the pitching coach, Billy Conners, went over the signs with the pitchers, then asked if there were any questions, Maddux snapped, "Yeah, you didn't show us the sign for the brushback."

Conners recalled his first impression of Maddux as that of a young kid with the makings of an outstanding pitcher. Conners remembered he was mentally tough, would knock you off the plate, knew what he was doing, but could not overpower hitters.

"You're going to need a cut fastball," the coach told Maddux, "to break in to a left-handed batter."

Maddux struggled in 1987, often making a mistake common to young pitchers. He tried to get by mainly on his fastball. Many young pitchers think the way to get out of trouble is by throwing harder. They begin to overthrow. That had worked in the minors, but big league hitters ate it up. Maddux won 6 and lost 14, and was sent down to Iowa in August.

The Cubs had a new pitching coach, Dick Pole. Pole took Maddux to Maracaibo in the Venezuelan winter league to teach him that he could do better when he was in a jam by throwing softer, not harder, using a changeup or slow curve.

"That was the turning point in his success," Pole said.

Maddux agreed. "I lost enough games trying to put more on the ball, so finally I said maybe I should try to take more off. If you get beat enough trying to do something, you eventually change." He also mastered the cutter that Conners had showed him.

In 1988 Maddux was 15–3 when he made the All-Star team for the first time. He finished the year with an 18–8 record, won 19 the next year, then 15 in 1990 and 1991. The Cubs won the NL East in 1989, but Maddux was hit hard in his two starts in the playoffs against the San Francisco Giants, and the Cubs went home early.

In January 1989 Maddux married his high school sweetheart, Kathy, in Las Vegas.

Maddux credits Cubs pitching coach Dick Pole for making him a winning pitcher. Pole took him to Venezuela one winter and taught him how to throw a changeup. "That was the turning point in his success," Pole says.

Maddux worked on his fielding and hitting as fervently as his pitching. He realized that those skills could help him win games. When he threw on the side between starts, it was always to work on something he felt needed improving.

Maddux never let up on himself. When he won, he felt like, "This is my job. I'm supposed to do this." When he lost, it was, "I need to be better. Give me the ball. I want to go back out there tomorrow."

One day he won a game, 1–0. The pitching coach walked by and congratulated him. "I didn't pitch well today," Maddux replied. As soon as one game was over, he put it behind him and began planning his strategy for the next one,

He was still yelling at himself on the mound whenever he felt he had made a mistake. "But he was always in control," Conners said. "He never blew up. He'd yell, then turn and face the hitter as composed and focused as before."

By 1989 Maddux had become the "old man" the other pitchers looked up to and went to for help. He was 23. In pre-game meetings he would dispense pitching wisdom on how to work the hitters early and late in the game. During a game, he might say to a pitcher sitting beside him, "I would throw this guy this and that to make sure I get to that third pitch to get him out with."

Joe Girardi was a rookie catcher that year. When Maddux was not pitching, Girardi would sometimes turn to him for help. "In situations where I didn't know exactly how to get the hitter out, and the count was 2 and 2 or 3 and 2 and the batter had fouled off a few pitches, I'd look over to Greg in the dugout and he would give me a sign what to throw."

Maddux wanted to be the best pitcher and fielder and hitter; in fact, he wanted to be the best at everything: golf, card games, Jeopardy!, and especially Super Nintendo, which he took with him on road trips.

"I'd win sometimes," Girardi said, "but everything he does is with a very competitive nature. We had some real battles with Super Nintendo. On days he was going to pitch, it helped him by taking his mind off the game."

Maddux was so competitive, he even fought his own body. He began to have trouble with his eyes but refused to admit it. "He started crossing up the catchers because he couldn't see the signs," said Girardi. "He crossed up Hector Villanueva three times one night in New York.

The ball arrives too late for Cubs catcher Joe Girardi to tag Kevin McReynolds of the Mets. Girardi would play Super Nintendo with Maddux to help the pitcher relax on the days he was going to start. "We had some real battles," Girardi says.

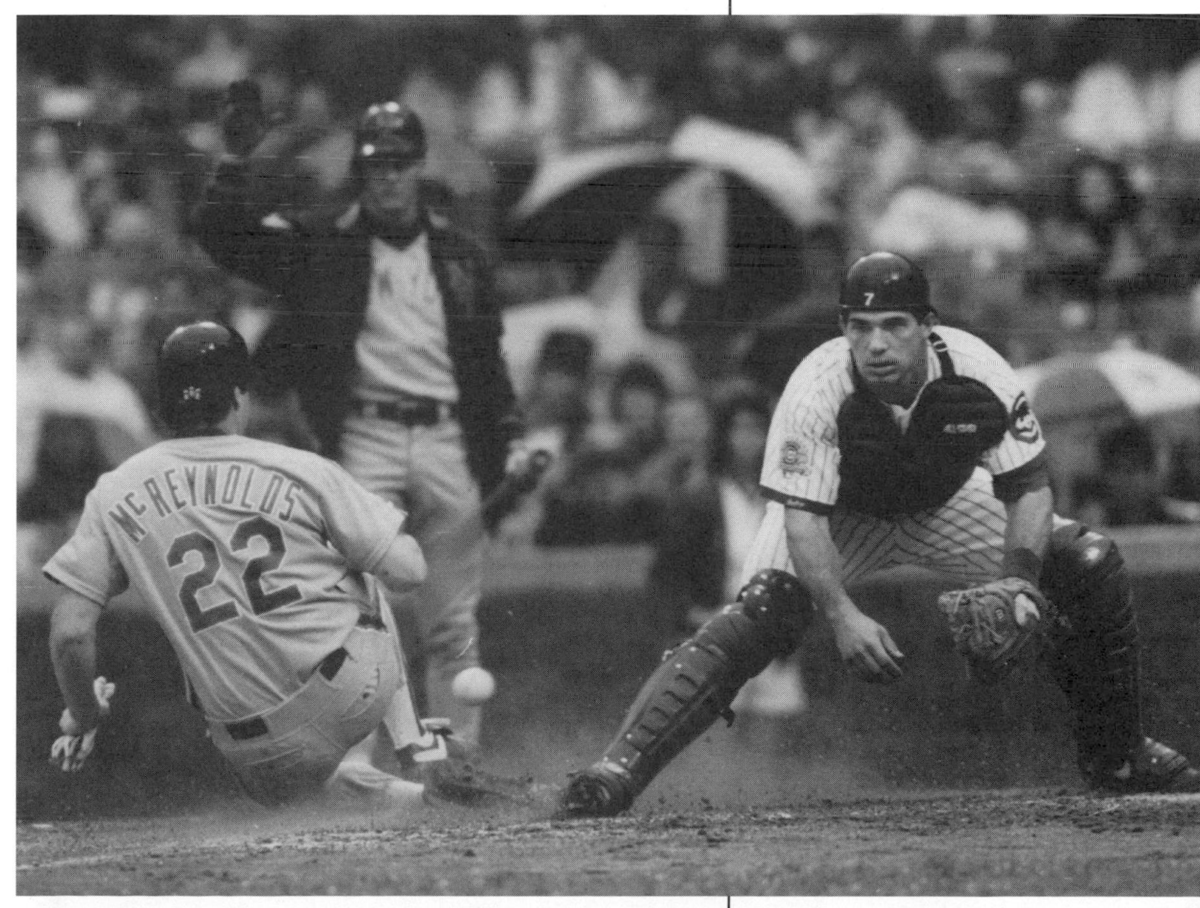

That can make a catcher nervous. He'd stand there squinting in at the catcher. We kept telling him, 'You're blind as a bat,' but he said 'No, my eyes are fine.' It was a couple years before he agreed to wear glasses."

With his glasses on, Maddux looked even more like an office worker. "When he puts his glasses on and sits cross-legged in the dugout," said Johnny Oates, "he looks like a docile, easy-going person. But he's not. He may look more like a librarian than an athlete, but when he takes his glasses off and puts his contacts in and goes to work, look out."

Asked to single out one game that best personified Maddux, several Cubs players cited September 5, 1992 against San Diego. Maddux went into September with a 16–10 record and a chance for his first Cy Young Award. He had time

Greg Maddux and his wife, Kathy, talk to reporters at Wrigley Field in Chicago after Maddux won the 1992 Cy Young Award, the first of four consecutive Cy Youngs.

for five or six more starts to reach 20 wins. "That day he put the team ahead of his own stats," they said, "and jeopardized his chances for the Cy Young."

In the seventh inning of a 3–3 game, the San Diego pitcher fired a fastball over Ryne Sandberg's head on an 0 and 2 count. The umpire then warned both pitchers against throwing at hitters. But Maddux was determined to protect his teammates with a payback, even if it meant being tossed out of the game and losing his shot at 20 wins. With two out in the top of the eighth, he drilled Padres catcher Dan Walters in the back, and was immediately ejected. Reliever Jeff Robinson gave up a home run to the next batter and Maddux took the loss. He won his last four decisions to finish at 20–11 and earn the Cy Young trophy. Maddux would go on to win four Cy Youngs in a row, but not with the Cubs.

6

THE AWESOME SEASON

"I could have pitched better."
— Greg Maddux

A free agent after the 1992 season, Greg Maddux wanted to stay with the Cubs. At home in Las Vegas, he expected to receive a contract offer from them, but they never called.

The Atlanta Braves offered him $28 million for five years. The Yankees offered even more. Before accepting any offers, Maddux called the Cubs and gave them a last chance to sign him. They told him they did not have the money. Maddux thought the Braves had the better chance of winning the World Series, so he accepted their lower terms.

Atlanta already had an outstanding pitching staff. Tommy Glavine, John Smoltz and Steve Avery were all proven winners. But for the past two years they had fallen short of winning a world championship. In 1991 they had led the Minnesota Twins 3 games to 2 in the World Series, then lost two heartbreakers in the Metrodome, 4–3 in 11 innings and 1–0 in 10. In 1992 they had lost to Toronto; the Blue Jays won two of the games in the ninth inning and one in the 11th. Each of their last seven World Series losses had been by one run. The Atlanta management felt that adding Maddux's arm would surely put them over the top.

Knowing that they could win games for him, Maddux works on his hitting and fielding as much as his pitching.

Atlanta pitching coach Leo Mazzone had a different approach to working his pitchers. He had them throw on the side twice between starts; most teams ask their pitchers to throw just once. The Braves' hurlers missed fewer starts than any other major league team.

Paced by Tommy Glavine, who won 22, and Maddux, who won 20, the Braves cruised to the West Division title with 104 victories. They produced a lot of runs, but not when Maddux was pitching; in his 10 losses they scored a total of 15 runs. His efforts were rewarded with his second Cy Young Award.

But the Braves' postseason jinx continued. Maddux won Game 2 against the Phillies in the NLCS, 14–3. The Phillies led, 3 games to 2, when he next started. In the first inning, a line drive struck him on the knee and hobbled him. He took a 6–3 loss and the Braves went home for the winter. For the third year in a row, they had fallen short, disappointing their fans and themselves.

Maddux hit a groove in 1994 that would continue for two unparalleled years. No other pitcher came close to his 1.56 earned run average in 1994. He won 16 and lost 6, completing 10 of his 25 starts. The players' strike ended the season on August 12, costing him another 10 starts. His third straight Cy Young was no contest.

"He was awesome," said Atlanta left-hander Kent Mercker. "He would talk on the bench about setting up hitters, but you learned from watching him. He seemed to know when a hitter was not going to swing and he'd throw one over the plate. And he'd know when a hitter was going to swing, and throw one a little out of the strike zone."

Maddux constantly studied the game to learn and improve. "We'd be playing cards," Mercker said, "and a game would be on television. He's playing and watching TV at the same time, studying pitchers, studying hitters, studying the game all the time."

Maddux's command and confidence on the mound helped players at other positions perform better. "The pitcher needs the guys behind him unless he can strike out 27 a game," said outfielder Mike Devereaux, the Braves' 1995 NLCS MVP. "Maddux is a fielder's delight because he throws strikes, works fast, has a plan and sticks to it. A slow or wild pitcher causes fielders to get flat-footed, and a ball can get through the infield by an inch that otherwise wouldn't. With every pitch the adrenalin flows and the fielders are on their toes. If a pitcher throws a lot of pitches, walks a couple guys, paces around between pitches, has a couple conferences with the catcher, the fielder can't get 'up' on every pitch after that.

"And if a pitcher has a plan but can't throw the ball where he wants it to go, that's trouble."

The players' strike continued into the 1995 season, delaying the start by three weeks. The Braves and their fans had high expectations. The players were constantly reminded by the media that they could win every game during the season, but if they did not win the World Series they would be considered failures. They had a powerful lineup, including Fred "Crime Dog" McGriff, David Justice and Chipper Jones. They had added an outstanding leadoff man in Marquis Grissom. They had the best pitching staff in baseball.

Players worry about sore arms, shin splints, and pulled muscles during spring training. But Greg Maddux came down with chicken pox, which he caught from his 15-month-old daughter, Amanda Paige. He made just one start that spring, but he took the ball on opening day, retired the first 11 batters he faced, and gave up one hit in the five innings he worked. As usual, his postgame comment was, "I could have pitched better."

The Braves breezed through the short season, winning 90 games and finishing 21 games in front in the NL East. Maddux had the finest season any pitcher ever had. He was as near perfect as a human could be. He rarely threw as many as 100 pitches in a game, seldom walked a batter, and almost never gave up a run. In 69 starts since the 1993 All-Star break, he had given up more than three earned runs only five times. He won 19 games and lost 2, walking only 23 batters all year. He once went 51 innings without issuing a free pass. He pitched 10 complete games and never lost on the road. While the average pitcher gave up more than four runs per game, Maddux surrendered 1.63. Amazed fans had to go back 75 years to find another pitcher who had been so dominating over two years—the legendary Walter Johnson in 1918–1919.

The Atlanta Braves pitching staffs of the 1990s rank among the best of all time. The starting five when Maddux joined them for spring training in 1993 were, from left: Tom Glavine, Maddux, Pete Smith, John Smoltz and Steve Avery.

But, as if to prove he was really human, Maddux came down with the flu in August and missed his first start in three years with the Braves.

In the first round of the playoffs, Atlanta faced the Colorado Rockies, one of the two teams that beat Maddux in '95. Playing the first two games in the mile high city of Denver, where home runs flew like popping corn, did not faze Maddux. "The best team has the advantage," he said simply. Maddux was not sharp in the opener; in seven innings he gave up two walks and a home run and hit a batter. But the Braves won, 5–4.

Four days later he was again not Maddux-sharp. The Rockies hit two home runs off him (he had given up only eight all year). But he won, 10–4.

Maddux beat the Cincinnati Reds in the final round, 5–2. After he walked two, hit a batter and threw a wild pitch, writers wondered if he was tired. But he returned to form with a masterful two-hitter in the first game of the World Series. He was unable to claim the championship victory in Game 5, losing 5–4, leaving it up to Tommy Glavine to win the clincher, 1–0.

For the second straight year Maddux was a unanimous choice for the Cy Young Award, becoming the first ever to win it four times in a row. He also won his sixth straight Gold Glove. In accepting the trophy, he thanked the coaches who had helped him the most along the way: Dick Pole, Billy Conners and Leo Mazzone. Then he went back to Las Vegas to disappear from the spotlight. He had no interest in the hoopla and the celebrity surrounding the game. He thrived only on the time between the first pitch of the game and the last.

"Everything else," he said, "you can have."

7

A NATIONAL HERO

"People wonder how Maddux does it."
— Don Zimmer

Greg Maddux and the Atlanta Braves became America's team in the 1990s. The Turner Broadcasting System, which owned the team, aired their games on Cable TV in all parts of the country. Many fans arranged their schedules so that nothing would interfere with their watching the Braves play when Maddux was pitching. "I want to be able to tell my grandchildren that I saw him pitch," was a common attitude from Maine to California.

Nobody has ever won more National League games—373—than Hall of Famer Christy Mathewson of the New York Giants 1901-1916. Matty pitched as much with his brain as his arm, outthinking hitters and delivering the ball exactly where he wanted it to go. Greg Maddux resembles Mathewson on the mound more than any other modern pitcher.

Maddux bore a striking similarity to a pitcher for the New York Giants who had become a national idol 90 years earlier: Christy Mathewson. Baseball fans then flocked to see Matty so they could tell their grandchildren that they had seen him. There was no radio or television at the height of Matty's fame in 1905, when he pitched three shutouts in five days in the World Series. Nicknamed Big 6 because he was a six-footer at a time when few players stood that tall, he was so famous a letter with nothing but a big "6" on the envelope was delivered to him in California.

There had been other phenomenal pitchers over the years: Lefty Grove in the 1920s and 1930s who, one writer said, "could throw a lamb chop past a wolf;" Sandy Koufax, another southpaw who could throw with the speed of lightning in the 1960s; Bob Gibson, who was so intimidating he once threw at a batter standing in the on-deck circle; and in 1995 Seattle's Randy Johnson, a 6-foot-10 left-handed bolt thrower who made left-handed hitters wish for appendicitis rather than have to face him.

But they were power pitchers; compared to the expresses they threw, Greg Maddux drove a horse and buggy. Former manager Don Zimmer said, "When you watch a Randy Johnson pitch, everybody oohs and aahs over his fastball. Nobody ever does that about Maddux. He just knows how to get you out. Koufax struck out everybody with pure speed. People wonder how Maddux does it."

Like Mathewson, Maddux pitched with his head as much as his arm. What the poet Ogden Nash wrote about Mathewson applied equally to Maddux:

M is for Matty,
Who carried a charm
In the form of an extra
Brain in his arm.

Both pitchers could throw the ball precisely where they wanted it to go most of the time. Mathewson once pitched 68 innings without walking a batter; Maddux went 51. In 17 years Matty averaged 1.59 walks per 9 innings; in the eight years beginning in 1988, Maddux averaged 2.21. In 1995 Maddux walked only 23 batters while winning 19 games. Mathewson is the only pitcher who twice won more games than the number of walks he issued in a year.

Ring Lardner, a writer in Matty's time, best described how Big 6 worked: "I bet he could shave you if he wanted to and if he had a razor blade to throw instead of a ball. If you can't hit a fast one an inch and a quarter inside and he knows it, you'll get three fast ones an inch and a quarter inside . . ."

Another story about Matty summed up both him and Maddux. One day a young player got three hits off Mathewson and boasted, "So that's the great Matty?"

"Do you know what kind of pitches they were that you hit?" asked an older player.

"No," the youngster replied. "Who cares?"

"Well, Matty does," the veteran said, "and you can bet you'll never get any of those pitches from him again."

Zimmer agreed. "There isn't a hitter who walks to the plate who doesn't have a weakness. But if a pitcher can't throw to that weakness, there's no sense knowing that weakness. Maddux both knew and could do.

"If a right-handed batter can't hit a slider on the outside two inches of the plate, and you can throw it there seven or eight times out of 10, you're going to beat that batter. If you can do it only three times out of 10, he's going to beat you. That's the difference between winning and losing pitchers."

Mathewson had no Nintendo games to play, but he was a checkers champion who could play several games at the same time, blindfolded. Maddux was almost unbeatable in card games, Jeopardy! or Nintendo.

Asked many times for the secret of his success, Maddux seemed coy and flippant in his simple replies. But he insisted that pitching is not complicated. Warren Spahn, the winningest southpaw in history, had boiled it down to: "Hitting is timing; pitching is upsetting that timing." Maddux did that by changing speeds.

Maddux said simply, "A fastball that moves, knowing where you want to throw it, and throwing it there, are the basics. Location is the key." He could throw five different pitches at different speeds to precise locations. He emphasized that a pitcher does not have to be big and strong enough to throw a ball 100 miles an hour to be a winning pitcher. "80 is fast," he said, "and 85 is plenty fast enough. If you can locate your fastball and change speeds, you can pitch. It doesn't matter how hard you throw if you can do that."

Lefty Grove dominated hitters in the 1920s and 1930s with the Philadelphia Athletics like Maddux would do 60 years later. But unlike Maddux, Grove did it with blinding speed; to the batters his fastball looked as small as an aspirin. Lacking that speed, Maddux "just knows how to get you out," said Don Zimmer.

Maddux was uncanny at getting inside hitters' heads and knowing what they were thinking, what kind of pitch they were looking for, and where they would hit the pitch he was going to throw. He seemed to know when they were going to swing and when they were not. Sometimes he would get a strikeout on a pitch that he did not intend to be a strike, but the bamboozled, over-anxious batter swung at it anyhow. He did this by talking to hitters and hitting coaches, watching batting practice, watching every pitch when he was not in the game—and remembering it all. On the mound, he noticed everything. If a hitter facing him changed his stance or his grip on the bat or the angle of his head, Maddux took it in. From these clues he deduced what to throw next.

The Yankees' leading hitter, Paul O'Neill, faced Maddux when both were in the National League. "Maddux would take a hitter out of his game," he said, "because he threw so many different kinds of pitches all for strikes. Even if you were not ordinarily a guess hitter, he would have you guessing what he was going to throw next."

Otis Nixon, a star leadoff batter, agreed. "He took me out of my game. As a leadoff batter, I would work the count, try to draw a walk, but I couldn't with him. I had to swing early or I might not get a pitch I could hit after that. I couldn't play my game. He did that to all the batters."

Atlanta catcher Charlie O'Brien summed it up: "As a hitter you're taught to get your pitch to hit. He didn't give it to you; he gave you his pitch to hit."

The key to changing speeds was to throw the changeup with the same arm speed and motion as a fastball, thus throwing off the batter's timing. Other organizations used tapes of Maddux pitching to teach their minor league pitchers how to do it.

During the winters, Maddux exercised his arm and shoulder using three-pound weights. He ran and rode the stationary bike. But his most important element in avoiding arm trouble was an unvarying delivery—the same windup, release point and stride on every pitch, the essence of good mechanics. "If all your mechanics are right," he said, "the ball has to go where you want it to go."

From 1988 through 1995 Maddux won more games—142—than any other pitcher, and averaged 254 innings pitched except for the strike-shortened years. Every time he took the ball, he expected to win. "He's got so much confidence he never thinks about failing," said O'Brien. "Very few guys can say that. He seems to become a better pitcher when he gets in trouble. When the game's on the line, he loves the challenge of facing the other team's best hitter. That's exciting to him. It all makes him the best pitcher in baseball."

8

NOBODY'S PERFECT

"He's a master."
— Yankee pitching coach Mel Stottlemyre

Expectations were high for Greg Maddux and the world champion Atlanta Braves on a cold, windy opening day in 1996. Before the game the Braves received their World Series rings. Maddux, warming up at the time, asked his father, Dave, to accept it for him. "I hope it meant as much to him as it did to me," he said later.

Although Maddux won the opener, reporters were shocked to discover that he was human and not perfect; he gave up four earned runs, something he had done only twice in 1995, and five times in 69 starts since mid-1993. By May, he was 4 and 2, and writers asked a question they would not have asked any other pitcher with a similar record, "What's wrong with him?"

When Maddux makes a mistake, he gets angry with himself, sometimes turning toward the outfield and yelling at himself with his glove in front of his face. And every time a batter gets on base, he considers that a mistake.

The only thing wrong with him was a little less luck, Maddux said. He knew that sometimes the ball would barely elude a fielder's glove or be fair or foul by inches. "It just shows how lucky I've been the last couple years. I got away with some mistakes last year that I haven't this year."

One day in August he gave up a grand slam after pitching eight shutout innings. In his next start he hurled six scoreless innings, then saw a fly ball hit the foul pole for a three-run homer.

After losing four in a row for the first time in four years, his record was 10–10 despite a 2.78 ERA. And again reporters asked, "What's wrong with Maddux?"

His reply: "Nothing." In his 10 losses the Braves had scored a total of 15 runs. But he expressed no frustration or disappointment and did not panic. His team was winning and that meant more to him than another three or four wins on his record. He continued to view videotapes of his games and study the hitters every day. He found no reason to change anything he was doing and finished strong, winning five of his last six decisions for a 15–11 record.

"Okay," said pitching coach Leo Mazzone. "He's not been awesome, just extremely good."

Only eight out of 100 National League starters won more than his 15; just one had a lower earned run average than his 2.72. Despite a persistently sore hamstring that hampered his running, he earned his seventh consecutive Gold Glove. It would have been a great year for any other pitcher; it was considered by some to be an off year for Greg Maddux.

Maddux walks back to the mound after giving up an RBI triple to Joe Girardi of the Yankees in a three-run third inning of Game 6 of the 1996 World Series. The Braves lost, 3–2, as bitter a loss as Maddux ever suffered; after losing the first two games, the Yankees won four straight to win the championship.

Braves right-hander John Smoltz won the Cy Young Award with a 24–7 record. The Braves had little trouble winning the NL East for the fifth year in a row. They swept the Los Angeles Dodgers in the division series. Maddux turned in a typical performance in Game 2: 2 runs, 3 hits, no walks, 4 fly ball outs. He faced 29 batters and threw 72 pitches, 14 of them called balls. The game was over in 2 hours 5 minutes.

But in Game 2 of the NLCS, the St. Louis Cardinals' Gary Gaetti rocked Maddux with a grand slam in the seventh to beat him, 8–3. Atlanta, down 3 games to 1, came back to take the next three. Maddux, returning to form, won the finale, 3–1, and the Braves faced the New York Yankees in the World Series.

Atlanta looked like a cinch to take their second straight world championship after they won the first two games in New York. Maddux was awesome in Game 2. He faced 29 batters; his first pitch was a strike to 23 of them. Most of New York's six hits were flukes. Only one fly ball out was hit in the 4–0 win.

"I've had games I might have pitched better," he said later. "But under the circumstances this is a game I'll take to the grave with me."

Lifetime .300 hitter Wade Boggs of the Yankees, referring to Maddux's magic tricks with the ball, called him the "David Copperfield of pitchers." Yankees pitching coach Mel Stottlemyre said, "If people want to learn something about pitching, they should watch [Maddux]. He's a master."

But the Yankees, with their own brand of team magic, won the next four games to dethrone the world champions. Maddux lost Game 6, 3–2, in the same way he had lost 11 games during the year: a masterful shutout except for one three-run inning, and a lack of offense by the Braves.

Disappointed but with head high, Greg Maddux returned to Las Vegas to play golf with his brother Mike and look forward to the next opening day, still confident that with a little luck and some runs behind him, he could pitch and win every time he took the ball.

CHRONOLOGY

1966	Born Gregory Alan Maddux in San Angelo, Texas on April 14
1984	Selected by Chicago Cubs in amateur draft
1986	Wins first major league start, 11–3, over Cincinnati Reds September 7
1992	Wins first of four consecutive Cy Young Awards; signs with Atlanta Braves as free agent
1995	Pitches two-hitter in first World Series start, defeating Cleveland, 3–2
1996	Wins seventh consecutive Gold Glove Award

MAJOR LEAGUE STATISTICS

CHICAGO CUBS, ATLANTA BRAVES

YEAR	TEAM	W	L	PCT	ERA	G	GS	CG	IP	H	BB	SO	SHO
1986	CHI N	2	4	.333	5.52	6	5	1	31	44	11	20	0
1987		6	4	.300	5.61	30	27	1	155.2	181	74	101	1
1988		18	8	.692	3.18	34	34	9	249	230	81	140	3
1989		19	12	.613	2.95	35	35	7	238.1	222	82	135	1
1990		15	15	.500	3.46	35	35	8	237	242	71	144	2
1991		15	11	.577	3.35	37	37	7	263	232	66	198	2
1992		20	11	.645	2.18	35	35	9	268	201	70	199	4
1993	ATL	20	10	.667	2.36	36	36	8	267	228	52	197	1
1994		16	6	.727	1.56	25	25	10	202	150	31	156	3
1995		19	2	.905	1.63	28	28	10	209	147	23	181	3
1996		15	11	.577	2.72	35	35	5	245	225	28	172	1
Totals		165	104	.613	2.87	336	332	75	2365.2	2102	589	1643	31
WORLD SERIES													
1995		1	1	.500	2.25	2	2	1	16	9	3	8	
1996		1	1	.500	1.72	2	2	0	15.2	14	1	5	
Totals		2	2	.500	1.97	4	4	1	31.2	23	4	13	

FURTHER READING

Inside Pitch Series. *Chicago Cubs.* New York: Bantam, 1993.

Goodman, Michael. *Chicago Cubs.* Mankato, MN: Creative Education, 1992.

Kramer, Sydelle A. *Baseball's Greatest Pitchers.* New York: Random Books for Young Readers, 1992.

The Sporting News Editors. *Baseball's Hall of Fame: Cooperstown, Where the Legends Live Forever.* Avenal, NJ: Random House Value, 1993.

Macht, Norman L. *Christy Mathewson.* Philadelphia, PA: Chelsea House, 1991.

INDEX

PICTURE CREDITS
Photo File: p. 2; AP/Wide World Photos: pp. 8, 13, 20, 39, 40, 42, 46, 56, 58; National Baseball Library & Archives, Cooperstown, NY: pp. 15, 34, 37, 52, 54; MGM Grand Hotel/Casino: p. 16; Dr. David K. Mulliken: p. 22, 26; Peoria Chiefs, Inc: pp. 28, 31, 32; Don Zimmer: p. 36; Transcendental Graphics: p. 48

NORMAN L. MACHT is the author of 25 books, 19 of them for Chelsea House Publishers. He is also the coauthor of biographies of former ballplayers Dick Bartell and Rex Barney, and is a member of the Society for American Baseball Research. He is the president of Choptank Syndicate, Inc. and lives in Baltimore, Maryland.

JIM MURRAY, veteran sports columnist of the *Los Angeles Times,* is one of America's most acclaimed writers. He has been named "America's Best Sportswriter" by the National Association of Sportscasters and Sportswriters 14 times, was awarded the Red Smith Award, and was twice winner of the National Headliner Award. In addition, he was awarded the J. G. Taylor Spink Award in 1987 for "meritorious contributions to baseball writing." With this award came his 1988 induction into the National Baseball Hall of Fame in Cooperstown, New York. In 1990, Jim Murray was awarded the Pulitzer Prize for Commentary.

EARL WEAVER is the winningest manager in the Baltimore Orioles' history by a wide margin. He compiled 1,480 victories in his 17 years at the helm. After managing eight different minor league teams, he was given the chance to lead the Orioles in 1968. Under his leadership the Orioles finished lower than second place in the American League East only four times in 17 years. One of only 12 managers in big league history to have managed in four or more World Series, Earl was named Manager of the Year in 1979. The popular Weaver had his number, 5, retired in 1982, joining Brooks Robinson, Frank Robinson, and Jim Palmer, whose numbers were retired previously. Earl Weaver continues his association with the professional baseball scene by writing, broadcasting, and coaching.